Harrogate As It Was

George Capel, A.L.A.

First edition May 1972
Second impression March 1978
Third impression April 1982

Published by Hendon Publishing Co. Ltd. © 1972. Hendon Mill, Nelson, Lancashire

Printed by Fretwell & Brian Ltd., Healey Works, Goulbourne Street, Keighley, West Yorkshire

Introduction

THIS is a book of photographs and prints, selected from local sources, showing Harrogate in the later decades of the 19th century and early decades of the 20th.

Annotation was made easier by the fact that many of the pictures were already excellently captioned. These have all been re-checked and additional information added where it would seem to be of interest.

Harrogate is fortunate in already possessing excellent accounts of its past: within the last twenty years we have had W. Haythornthwaite's 'Harrogate Story' (1954), H. H. Walker's 'Harrogate's Past' (1959), J. A. Patmore's 'An Atlas of Harrogate' (1963), and, most comprehensive of all, 'A History of Harrogate and Knaresborough' written by the Harrogate W.E.A. Local History Group, edited by Bernard Jennings (1970). The present volume, therefore, is not an attempt to *add* anything new to the history of the town but rather to convey visually the atmosphere and flavour of life in the Spa in those days. It is striking how much the face of the town has on the whole remained unaltered to the present day.

A view of High Harrogate engraved by J. Stubbs in 1829. This shows the Granby Hotel with the pond in the foreground

Another view of High Harrogate engraved by J. Stubbs in 1829. The Dragon Hotel is on the right of the picture.

DRAGON HOTEL existed in 1764 when the owners, called Liddal, won the Dunmow Flitch.* In early days it was also known as the Green Dragon. Between 1827 and 1830 it was in the possession of Thomas Frith, father of W. P. Frith, the painter. c. 1870 it became a boy's school, High Harrogate College, and was demolished in the 1880's to make way for Mornington Crescent. The New Inn, Skipton Road, became the present Dragon in the 1900's.

* *The Dunmow Flitch* was awarded to anyone going to Dunmow in Essex and swearing that for a year and a day they had never had a marital quarrel nor wished themselves unmarried. The custom is said to date from 1111 A.D.

ROYAL PUMP ROOM. This building dates from 1842, the first project of the newly-formed Improvement Commissioners being to provide a suitable building to house the sulphur well. It was designed by Isaac Shutt and cost £3000. The previous cover over the well was removed to the Tewit Well where it still stands. In 1842 the number of drinkers was 3,778; in 1867, 11,626; in 1925, 259,000. The Pump Room has been the museum since 1953.

TEWIT WELL shown here was discovered in 1571 by William Slingsby "who on drinking this water found it in all things to agree with those at the Spaw" (meaning Spa in Belgium).

THE GRANBY was formerly known as the Sinking Ship and the Royal Oak. The latter was its name in 1736 when Blind Jack of Knaresborough played the fiddle there. In 1788 Mrs. Wilks, the owner, built the theatre which stood in Church Square (now a private house); previously to this, touring companies had played in the Granby barn.

In 1795 it was known as the Granby (after the Marquis of Granby who had won fame in the Seven Years' War).

The present building was in existence in 1821 and has been much enlarged since.

The OLD SWAN was established c. 1700, rebuilt in 1820, became the Harrogate Hydropathic establishment in 1878 and reverted to its old name in 1952.

Some of the windows in the present building may be 18th-century.

These attractive prints were sold by T. Hollins, bookseller, printer and stationer of 26, Park Parade. He also published guide books of the town during the latter half of the 19th century.

OLD ST. MARY'S CHURCH before the laying-out of the Belmont Estate. It stood on St. Mary's Walk, which is shown in the course of erection.

Built in 1825 to serve the growing population of Low Harrogate, the chancel was added in 1865.

Replaced by present Church in West Cliffe Grove in 1916.

ROYAL SPA CONCERT ROOMS and Gardens, which stood next to the Royal Hall on site of present car-park. Built in 1835 as the Royal Promenade and Cheltenham Pump Room (the waters in this area had been thought to be similar to those at Cheltenham), by John Williams. The 6 acres of grounds included a boating lake and skating rink. The iron and glass pump room and colonnade were built in 1870. The rooms were acquired by the Corporation in 1896 and demolished in 1939. The pillars survive in a woodland setting in the Northern Horticultural Society's gardens at Harlow Car.

THE WHITE HART HOTEL dates from 1846. According to Professor Pevsner, "easily the best building in Harrogate". This photograph shows it in 1869.

THE QUEEN HOTEL, probably the oldest hotel in the town, may date from as early as 1660. Its first name was the Queen's Head (possibly Charles II's Queen, Catherine of Braganza).

The present building dates from 1855, was enlarged in 1861 and is now the premises of the Leeds Regional Hospital Board.

THE CROWN shown below, was established in 1740 by Joseph Thackwray, great-uncle of the owner of the Montpellier Square and Gardens of the same name. It was rebuilt in 1847, with additions to the east in 1870.

Adjacent to the Sulphur Well and the many other springs in the neighbourhood, the prosperity of the Crown reflected the changing fortunes of High and Low Harrogate, the latter's being on the ascendant. Lord Byron stayed here in 1806.

Royal Parade to the left was laid out in 1846.

A Meet of the Hounds in Low Harroagte opposite the Crown Hotel, about the year 1865.

THE PRINCE OF WALES was established at the main turnpike cross-roads (Otley-Knaresborough, Leeds-Ripon) about 1815. First known as Hattersley's, in the 1830's it became the Brunswick. It was rebuilt in 1860 and given its latest name in 1866. Now Prince of Wales Mansions.

In 1845 the first railway station took its name from the hotel. The Brunswick Station terminated a branch of George Hudson's York and North Midland railway.

N.B. Old signpost on right.

Mrs. Brogden's woolshop stood on the site of the bottom of Valley Drive, prior to the making of the Valley Gardens in 1887.

VICTORIA PARK UNITED METHODIST FREE CHURCH. Built in 1865, now demolished

Victoria House, the Co-op store, now stands on the site.

Viewed from Albert St./Station Parade corner.

HARLOW MANOR HYDRO was originally a private house built by a Leeds architect, John Milling, for himself in 1875. In common with the Cairn and the Harrogate Hydro (formerly the Swan), it combined treatment and hotel facilities under one roof.

It opened as a hydro in 1893, providing "Turkish, Russian, electro and chemical and needle showers, hot and cold plunges and medicated baths of every description".

NEW VICTORIA BATHS. Opened in 1871; their upper portion occupied by the Council Chamber and Municipal Offices until their replacement by the present-day Municipal Buildings in 1931 on the same site.
(The original Victoria Baths, 1832, had been built on the site of Cresecent Gardens by John Williams, owner of the Cheltenham Pump Room).

QUEEN VICTORIA'S JUBILEE, June, 1887. Mr. Samson Fox, who was later Mayor from 1889-1892, provided an ox-roasting on High Harrogate Stray.

The first drivers for the Corporation, photographed in 1882 at the stables, Market Square. Messrs. Henry Morland, Dick Richmond, Jackson Teasdale, Jim Clark, Tom Wade and Tom Waddington.

PRINCE ALBERT VICTOR, DUKE OF CLARENCE, visited the town on July 18th, 1889, to open the new Royal Bath Hospital.

Decorations in the town included triumphal arches; this one was erected near the railway bridge on Skipton Road.

VALLEY GARDENS, opened in 1887.

In the centre, the small "Gothick" pump room housing the Magnesia Well.

In the background, the newly-built Royal Bath Hospital which was opened in 1889 by Prince Albert, Duke of Clarence. £36,000 was raised by public subscription to pay for it.

The photograph on the right shows the earlier building. The hospital was founded in 1824 "for the relief of poor persons whose cases require the use of the various mineral waters and baths of Harrogate".

Three views of the PROSPECT PLACE area about 1890.

On the left looking south (somewhat less traffic than today).

Below Prospect Place and Crescent before the building of the "Pierhead" and Gardens.

The photograph on the opposite page shows a bath-chair rank. (At that date hire costs were 1s. 3d. for the first hour and 4d. for every succeeding quarter.

The Prospect Hotel dates from 1859, with enlargements in 1870.

St. Peter's Church from 1871; it was without its tower until 1921.

F.F&Co.

LOW HARROGATE about 1890. The Victoria Inn, left of centre, which stood at the bottom of Cold Bath Road, now demolished.

BIRK CRAG in the 1890's. A favourite walk of about 2 miles from the town through the Valley Gardens and over Harlow Moor, which all eventually came under the control of the Council.
William Grainge described it thus in 1871: "The grandest piece of scenery in the neighbourhood . .. On a fine day, when the heath is in bloom with the sunshine streaming over it, thick woods rising darkly on the west; the brook stealing into view from under an arcade of foliage and winding along the bottom in graceful curves—it forms a picture at once wild, grand and beautiful".

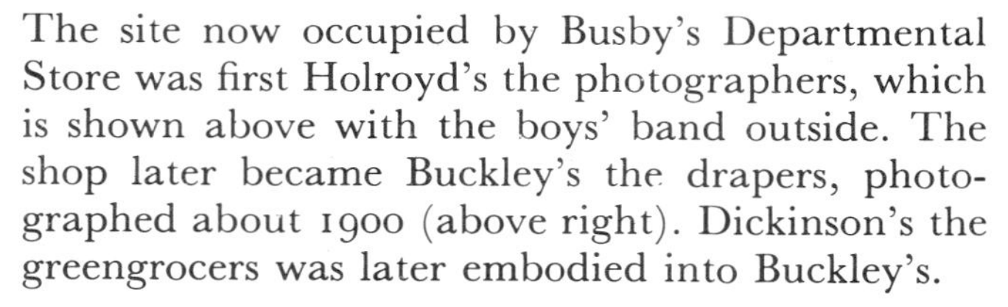

The site now occupied by Busby's Departmental Store was first Holroyd's the photographers, which is shown above with the boys' band outside. The shop later became Buckley's the drapers, photographed about 1900 (above right). Dickinson's the greengrocers was later embodied into Buckley's.

THE CAIRN HOTEL began life in 1890 as the Cairn Hydropathic.

In 1896 £2. 9s. od. to £3. 10s. od. per week paid for bed, attendance, table d'hote, breakfast, luncheon, afternoon tea, dinner *and* free bath each morning.

A weekly journal, the "Cairn Times" was published.

MONTPELLIER GARDENS before 1897 when the Royal Baths were built on this site.

WEST PARK STRAY about 1890.

Victoria Avenue Congregational Church was built in 1862.

"Belvedere" opposite, a Victorian villa, dates from 1861—a banker's residence, now the School of Art.

The fine terrace adjacent is early 19th century.

A hybrid form of transport for a hybrid business, about 1890: A caravan which stood in Skipton Rd. The small vehicle with chimney on the left sold hot peas and was named "The Enterprise".

MONTPELLIER BATHS. Laid out in 1835 by Joseph Thackwray, owner of Montpellier Gardens and the Crown Hotel and its estate, which included a number of sulphur springs. Their rivals were William's Victoria Baths; in 1839, 6000 baths in the season at the Montpellier; 4000 taken at the Victoria. The Baths were replaced by the Royal Baths and Winter Gardens, 1897.

ROYAL BATHS AND WINTER GARDENS—Stonelaying, July 10, 1894; completed 1897.

Two views of the Royal Baths.

On the left is the Kursaal. Here great artistes including Kreisler, Paderewski, Pavlova, Bernhardt and Melba performed before 1914. During the Great War it's present name—Royal Hall—was adopted.

HORSE CHARABANCS run by Burgess' Livery Stables, White Hart Mews, were much in demand in the summer for excursions. Four-in-hands, brakes and tandems were also run or hired.

VALLEY GARDENS, about 1900.
The Bandstand.

PARK PARADE, about 1900, with gas lamps. Previously named Paradise Row.

Christ Church dates from 1829, replacing an earlier chapel built in 1749. The transepts and chancel were added in 1861.

OXFORD STREET around 1900.

This is one of the earliest roads in Harrogate. It was called Chapel Street from the 1830's. This originally formed part of Chapel Road which connected Low Harrogate (probably leading from near the Crown) to Harrogate Chapel, now Christ Church in High Harrogate.

Houses which used to stand in the yard of the Ship public house (1837) before their demolition about 1900.

NB: refreshments available and prices.

The building of the MAJESTIC in 1900 (seen here on June 20th, 1924—one of the worst fires seen in Harrogate), and the GRAND in 1903 proclaimed Harrogate's national and international status.

This horse-drawn 'bus was run by Robert Dent, 14 Mayfield Grove, between Harrogate and New Park. Photograph about 1900.

J. Brown's, Saddlers, was in Oxford St., now Messrs. Pollard's, Cleaners.

This photograph was taken at the time of celebrations for the Coronation of Edward VII in 1902.

Otto Schwarz's Touring Band in Low Harrogate, 1903.

JAMES STREET in the 1900's.

Little change since then in the actual buildings. It dates from the early decades of the 19th century, its name being taken by tradition from James Franklin who owned land in this area (hence Franklin Mount and Road).

Like Parliament Street, this street began life as a residential area, later becoming a shopping centre. (Standing's dates from 1883).

ROYAL PARADE before 1913.

These buildings date from the middle of the 19th century. The chemist's shop still exists.

1909: The first motor charabanc excursion from Harrogate.

EARLY MOTOR TRANSPORT.

This is a motor driven coal cart from a photograph taken between 1908 and 1912 by Mr. H. Buckle.

The engine was built between the original shafts of a horse-cart. The steering wheel can just be seen, the driver being hidden.

Licensing the first taxicabs, May 11th 1908.

END OF AN ERA: Procession to the Memorial Service for Edward VII, May 20th, 1910.

Crescent Gardens, May 1910.

The occasion was the proclamation of George V outside the Royal Baths.

To the right, the fine Doric portico of the Spa Concert Rooms.

The German-British motor tour passed through Harrogate in July 1911. Prince Henry of Prussia was a competitor.

The photograph shows an entrant at the entrance to the Majestic.

A coach and four on The Stray, August 1911.

The Stray, 200 acres of open grassland, describes a half-circle south of the town centre from Low Harrogate to High Harrogate. It was secured for the recreational use of the inhabitants of the town when the Enclosure Acts in the 1770's were passed, the Stray being set aside for perpetuity as common land with free rights of access to everyone. Control was at first by "Straygate owners" who held the grazing rights. In 1893 the Corporation gained control of the Stray by purchase at a cost of £11,780.

AN AIR-RACE, with prize of £10,000, began from Brooklands on July 22nd, 1911. Harrogate was the end of the second stage, which started from Hendon.

The 'planes landed on the Stray between the Leeds and Wetherby roads.

An English pilot, Valentine, won Harrogate Chamber of Trade's tea-service for the first pilot to arrive at Harrogate from Hendon.

Visit of the Lord Mayor of London, June 8th, 1913, showing State Coach passing through Station Square.

STATION SQUARE during the First World War. Iron railings around station and carriage rank. The Victoria monument dates from the 1887 Jubilee, that part of the town then being considered as the Town Centre. Proposals were made to build a Town Hall on the land adjacent to the Library.

Valley Gardens. One afternoon in 1916.

"Before lunch" band. Royal Baths' Gardens, 1916.

VALLEY GARDENS, June, 1919.
Tea house with thatched roof.

1919: PEACE CELEBRATIONS.
One of the few photographs to show less affluent members of the community.

UNVEILING OF WAR MEMORIAL—September 1st, 1923 in the presence of Princess Mary and Viscount Lascelles.

PALM COURT!—The Winter Gardens in the Royal Baths in the 1920's—now the Lounge Hall.

1928. One of Queen Mary's frequent antiques-hunting visits to the town. Her daughter, Princess Mary, wife of Viscount Lascelles, lived near at Goldsborough Hall and later at Harewood.

PROCTER'S newsagents, Oxford Street, in 1926 at the time of the General Strike. (Fred Procter was responsible for many of the photographs in the collection).